Helen Marlais'
Succeeding at the Piano®
A Method for Everyone

For the Student

Throughout this book you will do many different activities such as:

Writing:

After you write the answers, you can play them on the piano.

Rhythm:

Just as this boy and girl walk in rhythm together, you will feel the steady beat in every rhythm activity!

Time to Compose:

Your very own compositions can be just as important as the pieces you learn.

Ear Training:

Learn notes and patterns in music by using your ears carefully.

Follow the Leader:

Use your ears to hear *rhythmic* patterns.

Parrot Play:

Use your ears to hear *musical* patterns.

Production: Frank J. Hackinson
Production Coordinators: Joyce Loke and Satish Bhakta
Editors: Joyce Loke, Edwin McLean, Peggy Gallagher, and
    Nancy Bona-Baker
Art Direction: Andi Whitmer – in collaboration with Helen Marlais
Cover and Interior Illustrations: ©2010 Susan Hellard/Arena
Cover and Interior Illustration Concepts: Helen Marlais
Engraving: Tempo Music Press, Inc.
Printer: Tempo Music Press, Inc.

ISBN-13: 978-1-56939-876-0

THE FJH MUSIC COMPANY INC.
Frank J. Hackinson

Grade 2A - Table of Contents

Review of Musical Symbols

Draw a line from the musical symbol to its correct name at each gate.
Then each horse can jump over every gate!

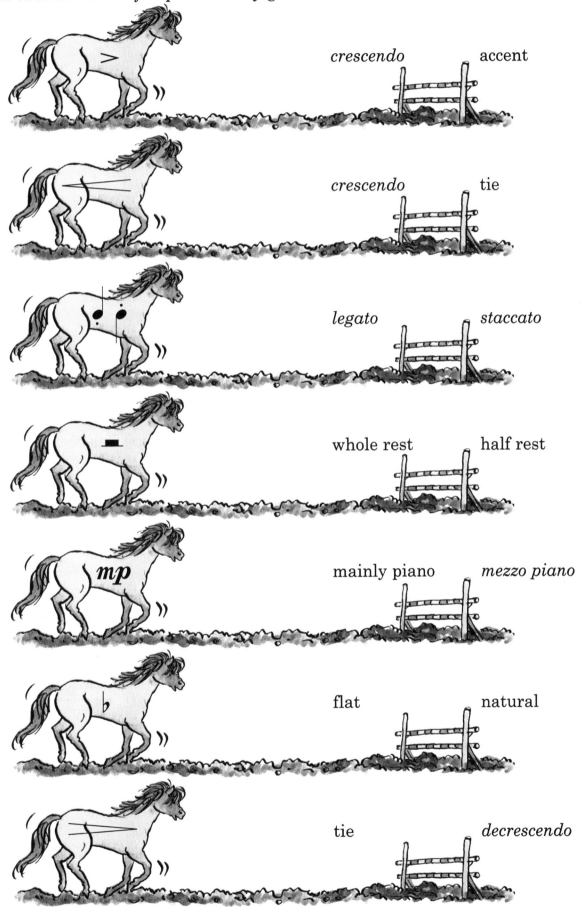

crescendo   accent

crescendo   tie

legato   *staccato*

whole rest   half rest

mainly piano   *mezzo piano*

flat   natural

tie   *decrescendo*

Eighth Notes (8th Notes)

Two eighth notes
equal a quarter note:

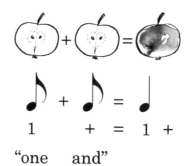

Two eighth notes are
usually beamed together:

Four eighth notes are
usually beamed together:

1
+ = 1 +
"one   and"

1. Draw a line from the notes on the left to the same total number of beats on the right. The first one has been done for you.

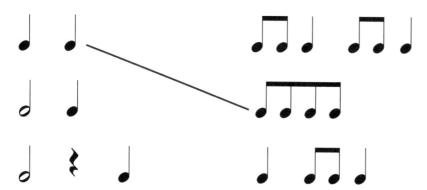

2. First draw the bar lines.
Then write in the counting. Write "+" for "and." The first measure has been done for you.
Clap and count aloud.

1 + 2 +

3. Write in the counting.
Clap and count aloud.
Then step in rhythm while saying the words.

Old King Cole

Old King Cole was a mer-ry old soul, and a mer-ry old soul was he;   he

called for his wife, and he called for his son, and he called for his fid-dlers three!

4

4. Add the time signature below.
Add in the counting. The first measure has been done for you.
Point to each note and count aloud, saying "1 and 2 and."
Point to the words and say them aloud.

Silverback

1 + 2 + 3 + 4 +
See the sil-ver-back by the tree! What an a-maz-ing ape is he!

Time to Compose:

- Make up a piece using the same rhythm as in *Silverback*.
- Will your piece be in 2/4, 3/4, or 4/4 time?
- Will it be in Middle C Position or C Position?

Parrot Play:

- Listen to your teacher play *Skip to My Lou*.
- Can you play the first phrase back by ear?
- Can you play the second phrase back by ear?

Skip to My Lou

Lost my part-ner, what shall I do? Lost my part-ner, what shall I do?

Lost my part-ner, what shall I do? Skip to my Lou, my dar-lin'!

❑ Check the box when you can play the first 2 phrases by ear.

REVIEW THESE TWO PAGES EVERY DAY AT HOME. PLACE A ✔ ONCE YOU HAVE FINISHED.

MONDAY	TUESDAY	WEDNESDAY	THURSDAY	FRIDAY	SATURDAY	SUNDAY

Review of Intervals and Notes from Bass G to High G

Say and play these Guide Notes:

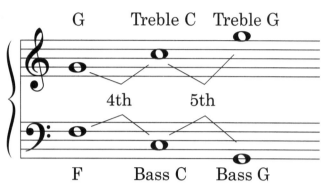

- Find and circle the Guide Note in every sea shell.
- Then fill in each answer before playing them.

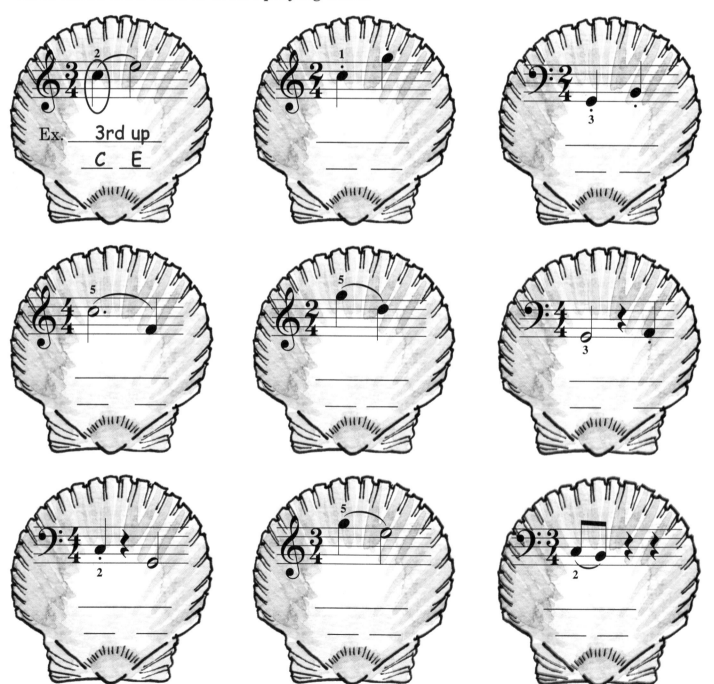

Ex.   3rd up
       C   E

FJH2061

Follow the Leader:

- Listen to your teacher clap the following rhythms.
- Can you clap them back?

1.

2.

3.

Ear Training:

- Your teacher will play intervals of a 2nd and a 5th.
- Without looking at the piano, name the interval you hear.

For teacher use:
(Play a, then b. Ask which was a 2nd and which was a 5th.)

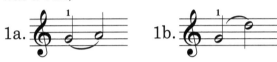

(Make up more if time permits!)

Ear Training:

- Your teacher will play either a or b.
- Point to and circle the one you hear.

Half and Whole Steps

- Write "H" for half step and "W" for whole step. Then write the names of the notes.
- Play all the notes on the piano.

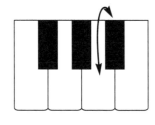

Ex. _____H_____

___A___ ___B♭___

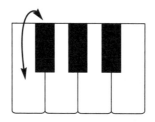

_____

_____ _____

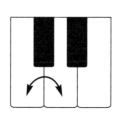

_____

_____ _____

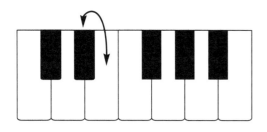

_____

_____ _____

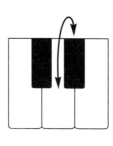

_____

_____ _____

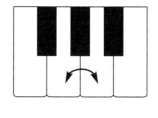

_____

_____ _____

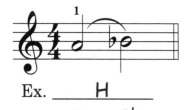

Ex. _____H_____

___A___ ___B♭___

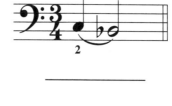

_____

_____ _____

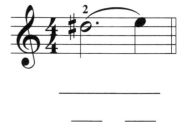

_____

_____ _____

_____

_____ _____

_____

_____ _____

_____

_____ _____

FJH2063

1. Help pack the suitcases for a trip!

- Draw a line from the **half steps** to the blue suitcase.
- Draw a line from the **whole steps** to the orange suitcase.
- Play all the notes on the piano as you go along!

2. Draw a **half step** higher from the given note. Add ♯, ♭, or ♮, if necessary.

 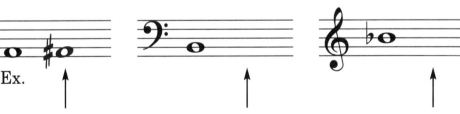 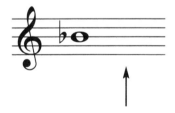 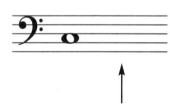

3. Draw a **whole step** lower from the given note. Add ♯, ♭, or ♮, if necessary.

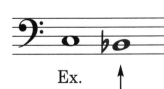  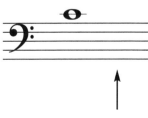 

UNIT 3

Spotlight on the Major Five-Finger Pattern

Whole Step	Whole Step	Half Step	Whole Step
W	W	H	W

1. Write the Major five-finger pattern in the boxes below.
Start each pattern by saying "Tonic" for the first note.
Then write the missing notes above the pattern. G Major has been done for you.

G Major:

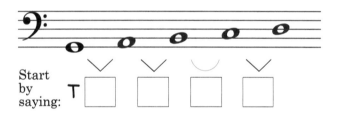

Start by saying: T

D Major:

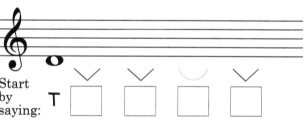

Start by saying: T

2. Circle the **tonic** (lowest note) of each triad. This tells you the name of the triad.
Then write the name of the triad on the line. Finally, play them!

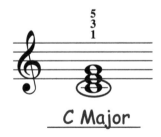

C Major

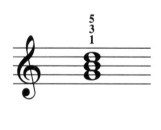

_____

_____

_____

_____

_____

_____

_____

FJH2063

In Search of Tonic (I) and Dominant (V)

- Draw a line from each spaceship to those planets which show the correct **tonic** and **dominant** notes. Some planets will be left out.

C Major   G Major   D Major

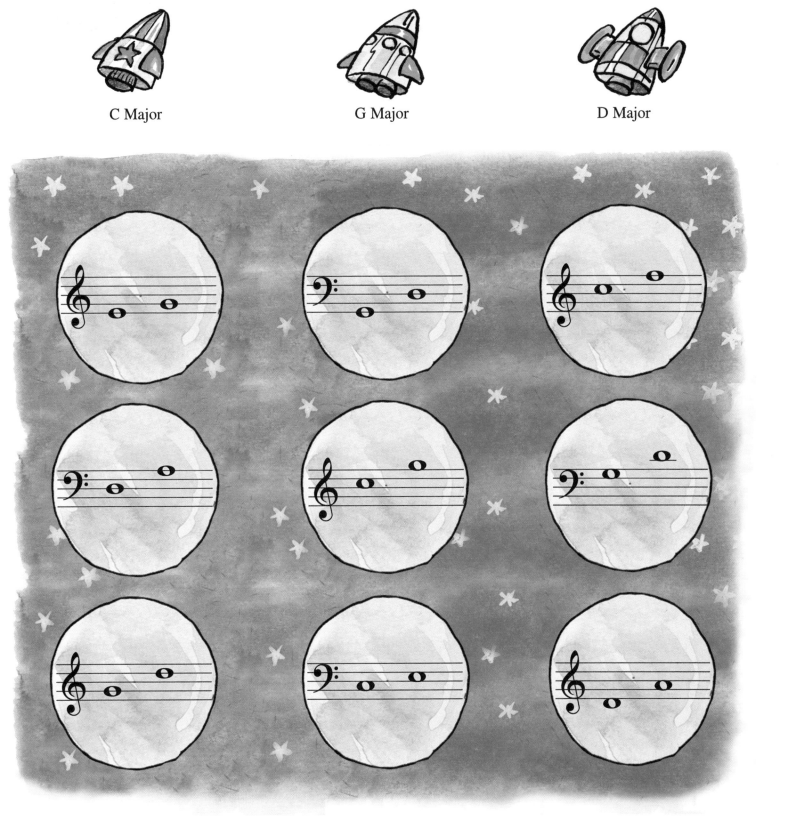

- Now play the planets with the I and V notes.

Transposing — Fun with Folk Songs

Yankee Doodle

- Play this phrase.

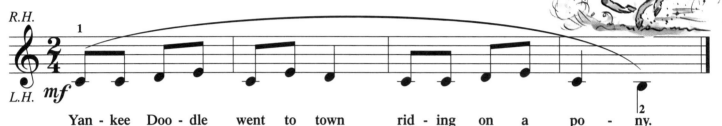

Yan - kee Doo - dle went to town rid - ing on a po - ny.

- Now transpose *Yankee Doodle* to D Major. (Use your ears! Some of the notes are missing!)

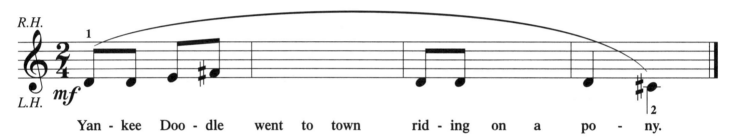

Yan - kee Doo - dle went to town rid - ing on a po - ny.

- Can you transpose the phrase to G Major?

Eency, Weency Spider

- Play this phrase in C Major.
- Then play the I and V notes in the L.H. on every downbeat.

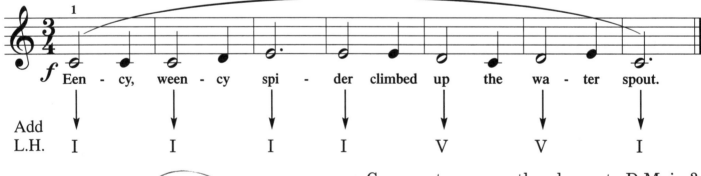

Een - cy, ween - cy spi - der climbed up the wa - ter spout.

Add
L.H.   I   I   I   I   V   V   I

- Can you transpose the phrase to D Major?

Time to Compose:

- Make up your own piece in G Major or D Major. Will it be in $\frac{2}{4}$ or $\frac{3}{4}$?
- Use I and V notes in your L.H. with the melody in your R.H.
- Be sure to start and end on tonic (I)!   My title: _____

Ear Training:

- Your teacher will play half steps or whole steps.
- In the spaces below, write "H" for half step or "W" for whole step.

1. _____ 2. _____

3. _____ 4. _____

5. _____ 6. _____

For teacher use: (To be played in any order.)

Parrot Play:

- How many phrases does *Tails* have?
- Listen to your teacher play it.
- Can you play the first two phrases back by ear?

Follow the Leader:

- Listen to your teacher clap a rhythm.
- Which one do you hear, a or b?
- Can you clap it back?

a.

b.

Tails

Traditional American

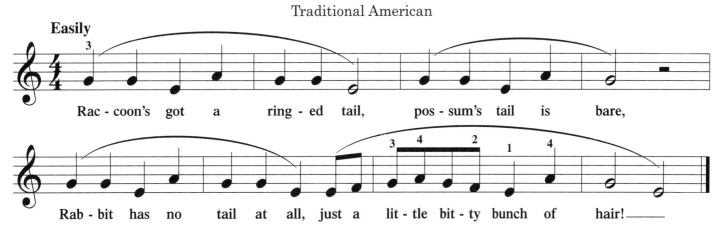

Rac - coon's got a ring - ed tail, pos - sum's tail is bare,

Rab - bit has no tail at all, just a lit - tle bit - ty bunch of hair!____

❐ Check the box when you can play the first two phrases!

Time Signature Review

- Add the time signatures below.
- Clap and count aloud.
- Then clap and say the words.

Giddy-up Donkey!

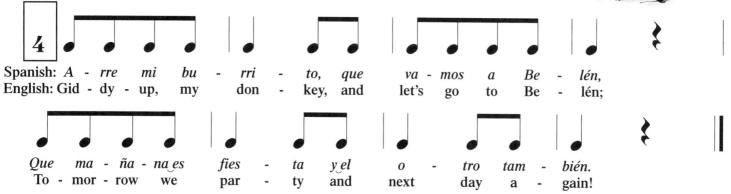

Spanish: A - rre mi bu - rri - to, que va - mos a Be - lén,
English: Gid - dy - up, my don - key, and let's go to Be - lén;

Que ma - ña - na es fies - ta y el o - tro tam - bién.
To - mor - row we par - ty and next day a - gain!

Star Light, Star Bright

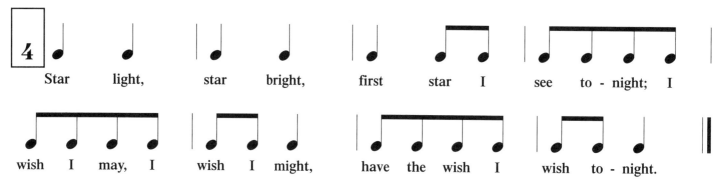

Star light, star bright, first star I see to - night; I

wish I may, I wish I might, have the wish I wish to - night.

Distant Drums

- Press down the damper pedal throughout.
- Tap the rhythm on the underside of the piano, under the keys.

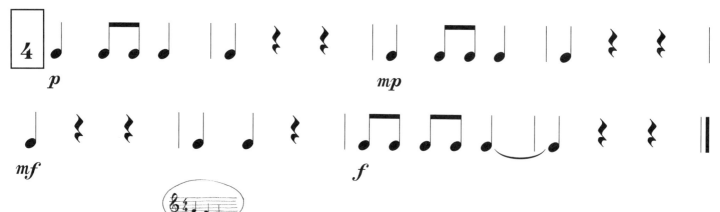

p   *mp*

mf   *f*

Time to Compose:

- Make up a piece using any of the examples above.
- Use the exact same rhythm.
- Use the C, G, or D Major five-finger patterns.

At the Competition

BEGIN HERE

For the blue ribbon, write the name and direction of the intervals.

For the red ribbon, draw the notes below.

For the gold ribbon, write the letter name of the notes below.

1.

   Ex. __4th down__

1.

   Ex. C♯

1.

   Ex. __B♭__ __E♭__

2.

   _____

2.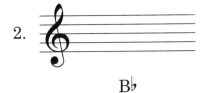

   B♭

2.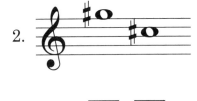

   __ __

3.

   _____

3.

   A♯

3.

   __ __

4.

   _____

4.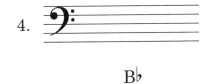

   B♭

4.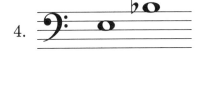

   __ __

5.

   _____

5.

   E♮

5.

   __ __

FIND AND PLAY **ALL** THE NOTES ON THE PIANO!

Ear Training:

- Your teacher will play a famous classical theme by Richard Wagner.
- Listen to the interval of a 4th in the first measure. Sing this theme to remember the 4th.

Here Comes the Bride

Here   comes the bride,   all   dressed in white!

- Your teacher will play the beginning of *Baa, Baa, Black Sheep.*
- Listen to the interval of a 5th between the first and second measures. Sing this melody to remember the 5th.

Baa, Baa, Black Sheep

Baa,   baa,   black sheep,   have you an - y   wool?

- Now listen to the intervals of a 4th and 5th again. Without looking at the piano, tell your teacher which interval you hear. (Sing the melodies above to help you.)

For teacher use: (Play a, then b. Ask which was a 4th and which was a 5th. Then make up more patterns for your students!)

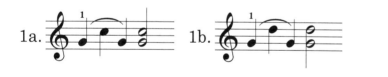

Parrot Play:

- Watch your teacher play a pattern of notes.
- Can you play each pattern back?

    For teacher use: (To be played in any order.)

FJH2063

UNIT 5

Major and Minor

MAJOR sounds BRIGHT.

MAJOR sounds HAPPY.

MINOR sounds DARK.

MINOR sounds SAD.

- Play the following melodies.
- Listen to the difference between major and minor:

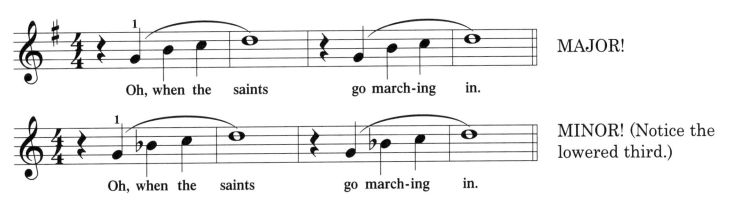

MAJOR!

MINOR! (Notice the lowered third.)

Is it MAJOR or MINOR?

- Play and sing:

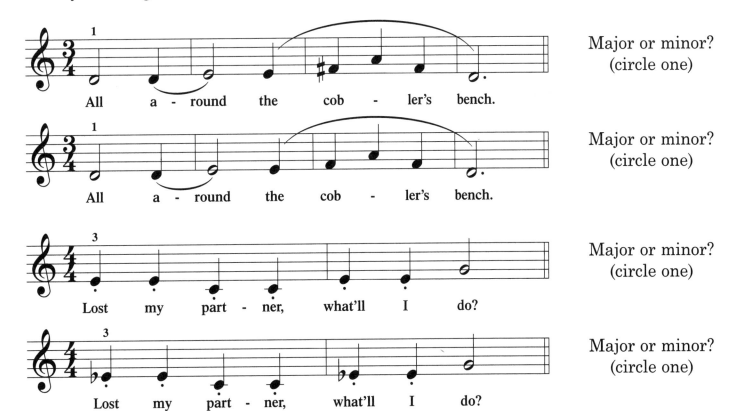

Major or minor? (circle one)

Major or minor? (circle one)

Major or minor? (circle one)

Major or minor? (circle one)

FJH2063

17

Major and Minor

- Play and sing the five-finger patterns below.
- "T" stands for "tonic" (first note).

G **Major** Five-Finger Pattern

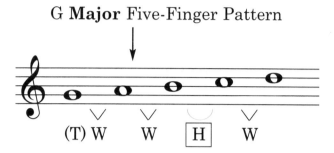

(T) W   W   H   W

- Write the **Major** Five-Finger Pattern:

(T) ____ ____ ____ ____

G **minor** Five-Finger Pattern

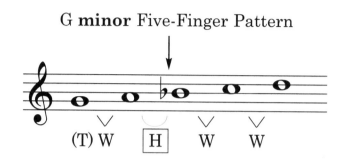

(T) W   H   W   W

- Write the **minor** Five-Finger Pattern:

(T) ____ ____ ____ ____

- Now write the notes of major and minor five-finger patterns. Mark the half steps and then play them.

C Major:

G Major:

C minor:

G minor:

Time to Compose:

- Create a piece using I and V in D in the L.H., shown below.

L.H.

- Your own R.H. melody above the L.H. accompaniment can be in either D Major or D minor. Make it AA[1] form.

Possible titles: *On a Ferris Wheel, At the Race Track*

My title: _____

FJH2063

The Major and Minor Fairies

Help the fairies change major triads to minor, and minor triads to major!

- In the empty staff next to each triad, write the new triad.
- Then play *all* the triads!

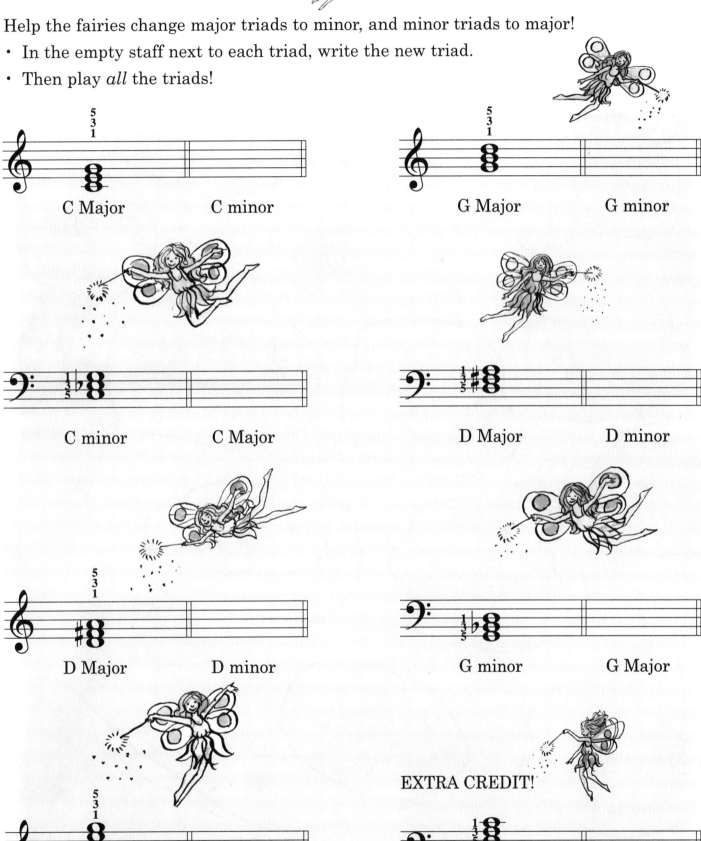

C Major   C minor

G Major   G minor

C minor   C Major

D Major   D minor

D Major   D minor

G minor   G Major

C Major   C minor

EXTRA CREDIT!

F Major   F minor

Rock Jumping

Help the boy jump to the rocks that are correct.

- Cross out the rocks that are incorrect.
- The path of **correct** rocks will lead the boy to the other side.

Major Five-Finger Pattern:
W W H W

Minor Five-Finger Pattern:
W H W W

C minor

G mino

D Major

2nd

C minor

Major 3rd

C minor

minor 3rd

G minor

20

FJH2063

Ear Training:

1. Your teacher will play two intervals in a row. One will be a Major 3rd and the other will be a minor 3rd.

Without looking at the piano, name the first interval, then the second interval. Write "M" for major and "m" for minor.

1. _____ _____   2. _____ _____   3. _____ _____   4. _____ _____

For teacher use:

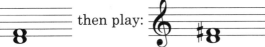

2. Your teacher will play two five-finger patterns in a row. One will be major and the other will be minor.

Without looking at the piano, name the first pattern. Write "M" for major and "m" for minor.

1. _____   2. _____

For teacher use:

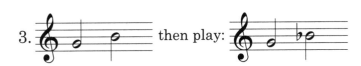

Low F

- Play these three Guide Notes in the Bass staff.
- Say each letter name aloud as you play.
- Then find the new note — Low F.
- It sits *below* the Bass staff.
- Low F is a _____ interval below Bass C.

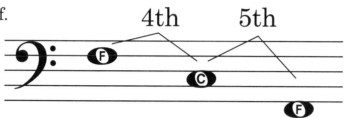

- Name the following intervals and notes.
- Then play the notes.

Ex. <u>2nd up</u>

<u>F</u> <u>G</u>

_____

_____ _____

_____

_____ _____

_____

_____ _____

_____

_____ _____

_____

_____ _____

_____

_____ _____

_____

_____ _____

Time to Compose:

- Create a piece using Low F.
- Use ABA form.

Possible titles: *The Giant and the Princess, Night and Day*

My title: _____

Space Shuttle Blast Off

• How long will it take you to answer these nine questions? Time yourself!

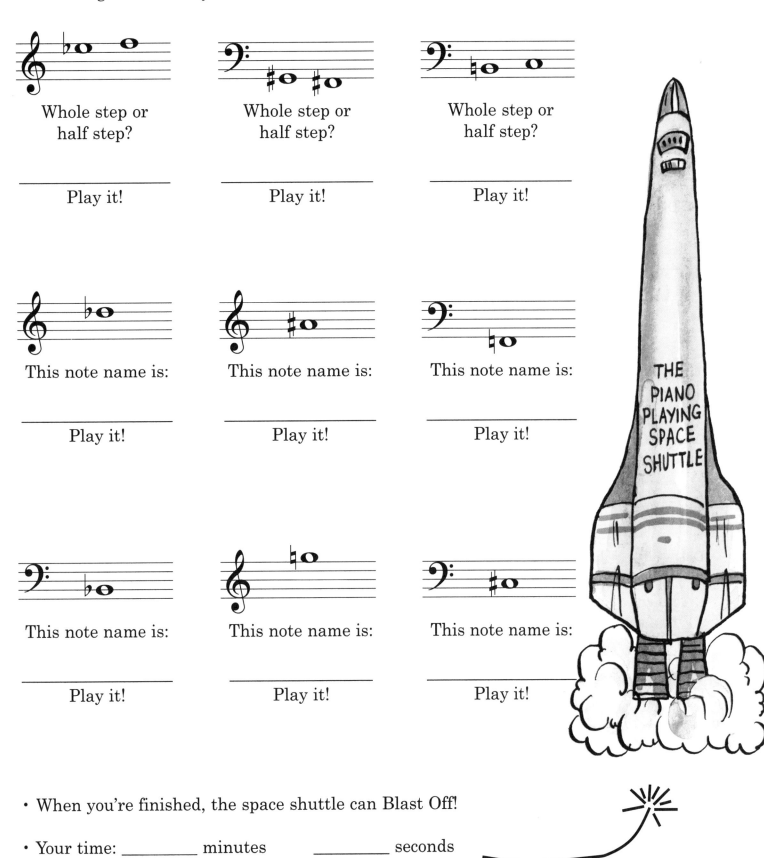

Whole step or
half step?

_____

Play it!

Whole step or
half step?

_____

Play it!

Whole step or
half step?

_____

Play it!

This note name is:

_____

Play it!

This note name is:

_____

Play it!

This note name is:

_____

Play it!

This note name is:

_____

Play it!

This note name is:

_____

Play it!

This note name is:

_____

Play it!

THE PIANO PLAYING SPACE SHUTTLE

• When you're finished, the space shuttle can Blast Off!

• Your time: _____ minutes   _____ seconds

Rhythm Review

- Add the time signature. Add the counting.
- Tap and count aloud while stepping to every ♩ beat.
- Tap and say the words while stepping.

Diddle, Diddle Dumpling

1 + **2** + **3** + **4** +

Did - dle, did - le, dump - ling, my son John,

He went to bed with his trou - sers on.

One shoe off, and one shoe on,

Did - dle, did - le, dump - ling, my son John.

- Write the counting under the notes.
- Place an X through the measures that have too many beats.
- Fix the measures by drawing in the correct beats and then clap and count aloud.

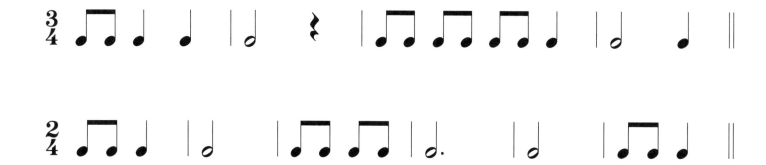

FJH206

Reviewing Low F through High G

Which note is which?

- Find and play these notes on the piano, starting from the lowest note and going to the highest note.
- Say the intervals between the notes as you play them.
- Listen carefully!

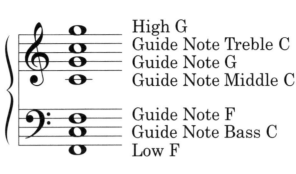

High G
Guide Note Treble C
Guide Note G
Guide Note Middle C

Guide Note F
Guide Note Bass C
Low F

Are you a

1. Write in the names of the notes, using the guide notes to help you. Then play the notes.

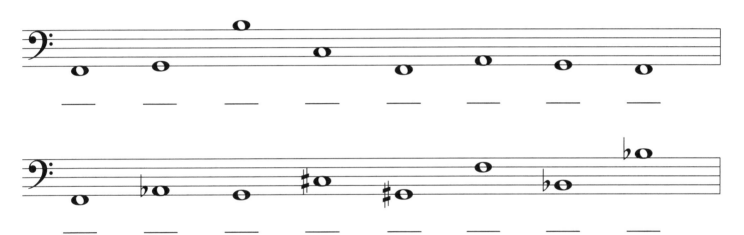

2. Notice the clef change! Write in the names of the notes. Then play them.

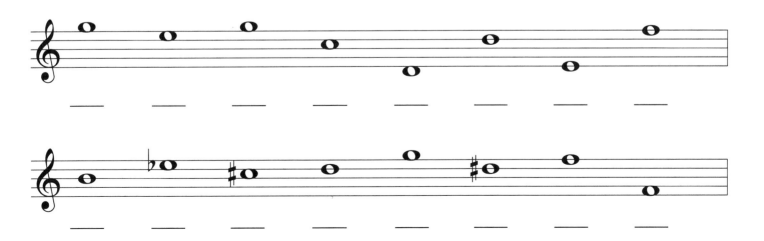

Follow the Leader:

- Listen to your teacher clap a rhythm.
- Can you clap it back?

For teacher use: (To be clapped in any order.)

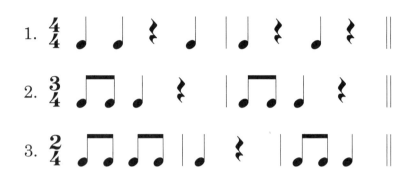

Ear Training:

- Your teacher will play a C Major five-finger pattern first. Then your teacher will play a 2nd, 3rd, 4th, and 5th, starting on C.

- Without looking at the piano, write the interval you hear.

1. _____   2. _____

3. _____   4. _____

For teacher use: (To be played in any order.)

Parrot Play:

- Your teacher will play *This Old Man*.
- Can you sing it together?
- Your teacher will play it again, and will play **one** wrong note.
- Point to where the wrong note is.

This Old Man

Traditional

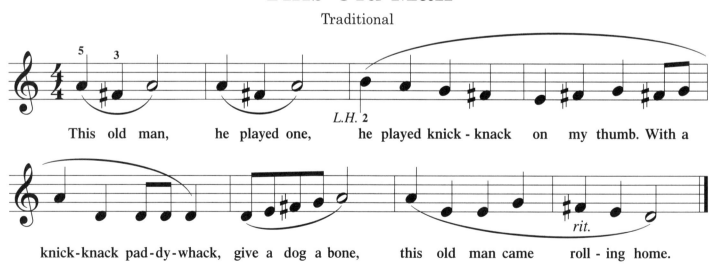

(For teachers: Experiment with a note change to see if your student hears the change.)

A Major and A Minor Five-Finger Patterns

1. The A Major five-finger pattern:

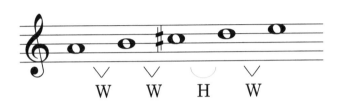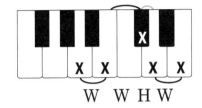

Write the A Major five-finger patterns below. Then mark the whole and half steps.

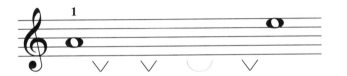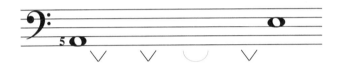

2. The A minor five-finger pattern:

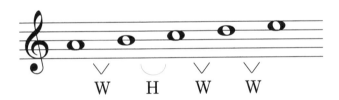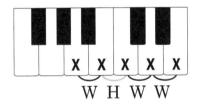

Write the A minor five-finger patterns below. Then mark the whole and half steps.

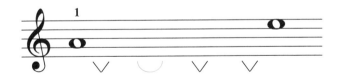

3. Now go back and label the tonic notes I and the dominant notes V.

It's Matching Time

Draw a line from the left to the correct answer on the right.
Then play all the triads on the piano.

1.   D Major triad

2.   G minor triad

3.   A minor triad

4.   A Major triad

5.   C Major triad

6.   G Major triad

Time to Compose:

• Make up a piece in A Major.
• The melody will be in the R.H.
• Use I and V in the L.H.   My title: _____

FJH2063

Totem Pole Notes

- One letter name below every totem pole is incorrect.
- Correct the letter names.
- Then play all the **totem pole notes** on the piano.

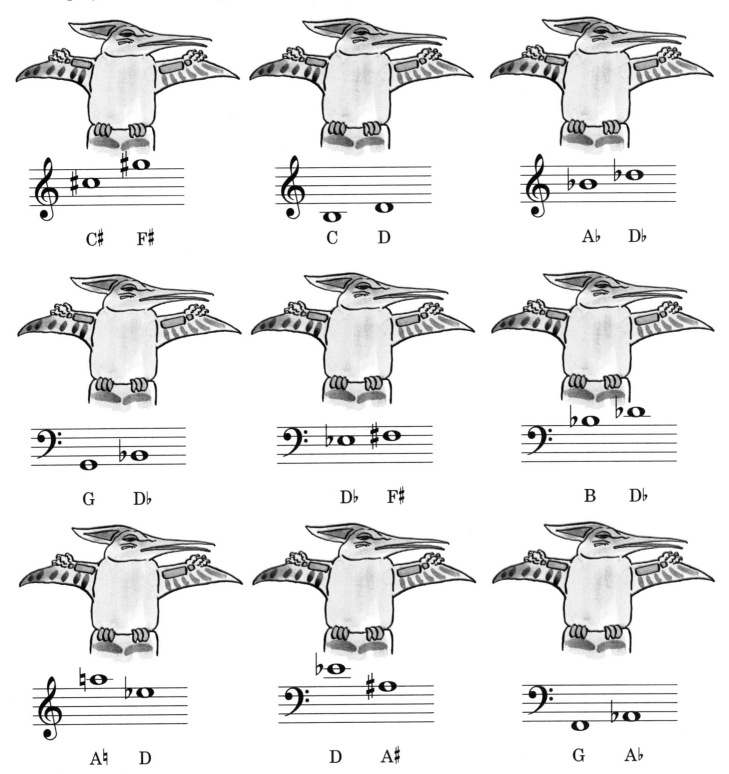

The Cyclops

The cyclops needs to find his anvil! If he takes the correct path he will find it.

• Draw a line from the cyclops to every correct answer.

Path #1	Path #2	Path #3

$\sqcap\sqcap + d = 4$ $d + \sqcap + \xi = 3$ $d. - \sqcap = 2$

$o - \sqcap + d = 4$ $o - \sqcap\sqcap = 2$ $\sqcap + \blacksquare + d = 4$

$d. + d. - \sqcap = 3$ $\xi + \sqcap + d = 3$ $d. + \sqcap - \blacksquare = 2$

In Greek mythology, a cyclop was a blacksmith. A cyclop lived underground and he worked so furiously that volcanoes would erupt into the air.

FJH2063

Parrot Play:

- Your teacher will play melodic intervals in A Major.
- Can you **sing** the intervals?
- Can you **play** them back?

2nd   3rd   4th   5th

- Now close your eyes.
- Your teacher will play the intervals above in **any order.**
- Write 2nd, 3rd, 4th, or 5th below.

1. _____   2. _____   3. _____   4. _____

Ear Training:

- Do you hear major or minor?
- Write "M" for major and "m" for minor.

1. _____   2. _____   3. _____   4. _____

For teacher use: (To be played in any order.)

(For teachers: In the "Parrot Play" exercises, have students review *Here Comes the Bride* and *Baa, Baa Black Sheep* on p. 16.)

Music Signs

Signs in music are like signs on the road.
They tell you where to go, how to go, and what to do!

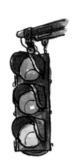

• Draw a line from the music signs to their correct meaning.

⌒   hold the note or rest longer

◁ (or *crescendo*)   play moderately loud, moderately soft

rit.   play a note sharp, flat, or natural

𝄐   gradually get softer

> (accent note)   gradually get louder

mf, mp   play smoothly

▷ (or *diminuendo*)   the end of the piece

♯ ♭ ♮   gradually slow down

‖   make the note louder than the notes around it

The Dotted Quarter Note ♩.

♩. gets one and a half beats. The ♩. is usually followed by an eighth note ♩. ♪

Clap and chant:

1 + 2 + 3 + 4 + 1 + 2 + 3 + 4 +

Both rhythms SOUND exactly the same!

Clap and chant:

1 + 2 + 3 + 4 + 1 + 2 + 3 + 4 +

- Write in the counting below. Two measures have been done for you.
- Swing your arm on every downbeat while counting aloud.
- Then play and count aloud.

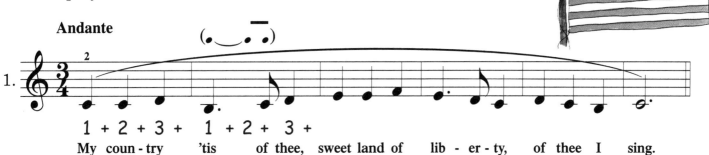

Andante

1.

1 + 2 + 3 + 1 + 2 + 3 +

My coun - try 'tis of thee, sweet land of lib - er - ty, of thee I sing.

Moderato

2.

Lon - don bridge is fall - ing down, fall - ing down, fall - ing down.

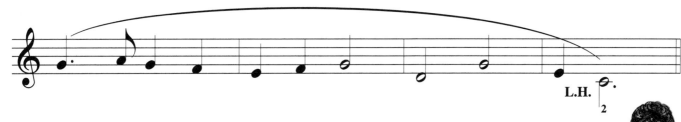

L.H.

Lon - don bridge is fall - ing down, my fair la - dy.

Time to Compose:

- Make up a piece using ♩. ♪. Use G or C minor.
- Will your piece be in ²/₄, ³/₄, or ⁴/₄ time?
- Add a 𝄐 at the end if you wish!

My title: _____

33

The Dotted Quarter Note Quiz

Your teacher will give you two points for each correct answer.

1. One measure is incorrect in each line. Fix it and then clap each line.

Points: _____

_____

2. Cross out the measure that has **too many** beats.

_____

3. Can you make the second line have the **exact same** rhythm as the first line? Play both lines. They should sound the same.

_____

Total points: _____ / 8

Teacher circles one: Great!

Good

Needs Work

34

FJH2063

Review of A Major

1. Add your choice of missing notes using notes from the A Major five-finger pattern. Then play the phrases.

2. Write the correct intervals in A Major. The first one has been done for you. Then play them.

upa3rd

upa4th

upa5th

upa2nd

downa5th

downa2nd

3. Circle all of the A Major triads. Then play **all** of the triads.

Expedition to the North

• Label the intervals and write the names of the notes below.
• Then draw a line from each pattern to the correct interval.

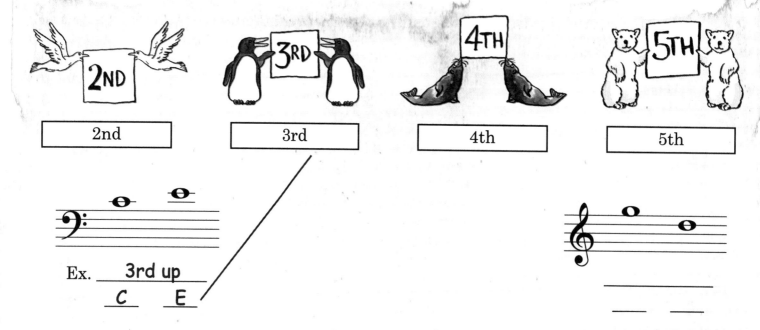

| 2nd | 3rd | 4th | 5th |

Ex. __3rd up__
       C   E

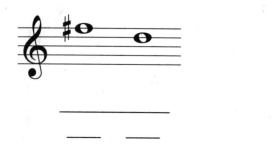

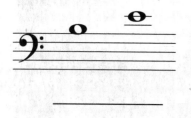

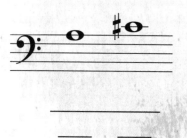

Now play all
of the intervals!

FJH206

Follow the Leader:

- Look at the music on the right.
- Listen to your teacher clap a rhythm.
- Can you clap it back?
- Circle the one you hear, a or b.

1a.

1b.

2a.

2b.

Ear Training:

- Your teacher will play *On the Bridge of Avignon*.
- Can you sing it together?
- Your teacher will play it again, and will make two mistakes.
- Point to where the mistakes are.

On the Bridge of Avignon

French Folk Song

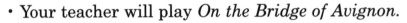

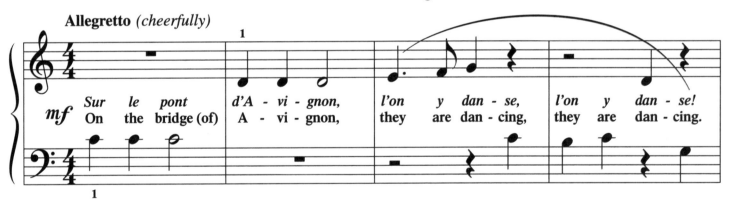

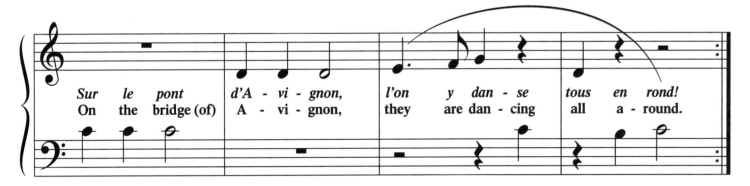

(For teachers: Experiment with rhythm or note changes to see if your student hears the mistakes.)

It's Matching Time

• Draw a line from each ladybug to the correct leaf.

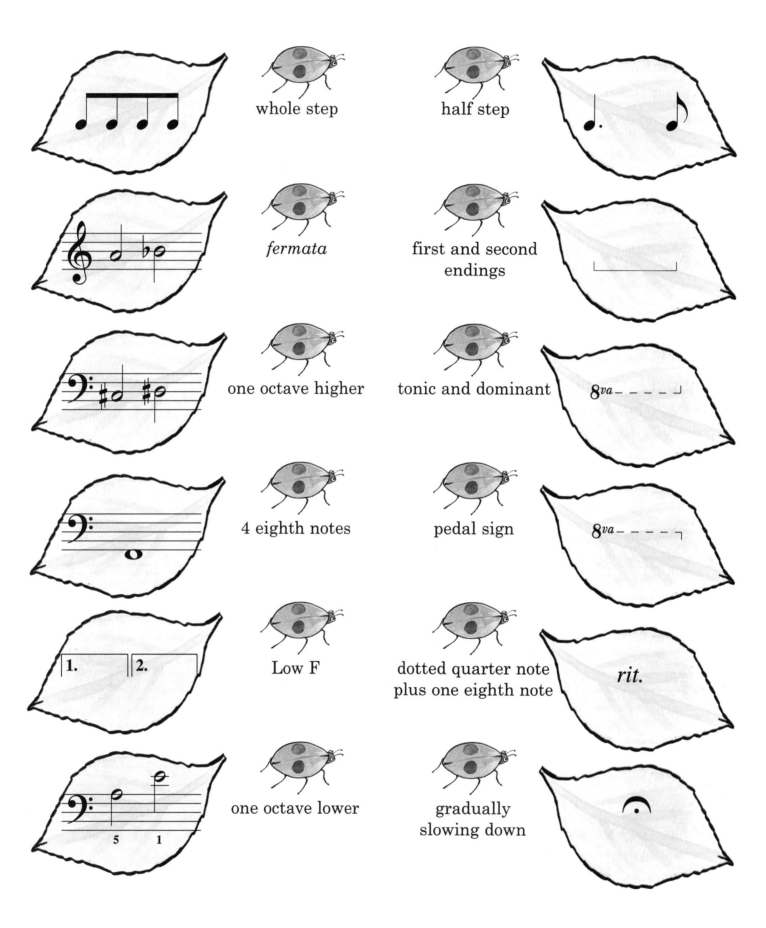

whole step

half step

fermata

first and second endings

one octave higher

tonic and dominant

4 eighth notes

pedal sign

Low F

dotted quarter note plus one eighth note

one octave lower

gradually slowing down

Hall of Fame—
Know the Composers

- You have played pieces by several composers in *Succeeding at the Piano*®. Some of their pictures are below.

- Rewrite their names on the lines. Can you say their names? (Your teacher will help you!)

- Choose one composer and tell your teacher something about him.

Papa Haydn

_____

Mozart

_____

Beethoven

_____

Schumann

_____

Bizet

_____

Chopin

_____

Brahms

_____

Vivaldi

_____

Certificate of Achievement

_____

Student

has completed

Helen Marlais'
Succeeding at the Piano®

Theory and Activity Book
GRADE 2A

You are now ready for
GRADE 2B

_____   _____

Date   Teacher's Signature

THE
F·J·H
MUSIC
COMPANY
INC.
Frank J. Hackinson